Little Pebble™

Community Helpers at School

by Mari Schuh

CAPSTONE PRESS
a capstone imprint

Little Pebble is published by Capstone Press,
1710 Roe Crest Drive, North Mankato, Minnesota 56003
www.mycapstone.com

Library of Congress Cataloging-in-Publication Data
Library of Congress Cataloging-in-Publication data is on file with the Library of Congress.
ISBN 978-1-5157-2400-1 (library binding)
ISBN 978-1-5157-2410-0 (paperback)
ISBN 978-1-5157-2416-2 (ebook PDF)

To St. John Vianney School —MS

Editorial Credits
Megan Atwood, editor; Juliette Peters, designer;
Tracy Cummins, media researcher; Tori Abraham, production specialist

Photo Credits
iStockphoto: Christopher Futcher, 11, kali9, 5, leezsnow, 19, Squaredpixels, 21, Steve Debenport, 7; Shutterstock: DGLimages, Cover, JPC-PROD, 15, michaeljung, 9, Monkey Business Images, 17, Natykach Nataliia, Cover Back, 3, 24, spaxiax, 1, wavebreakmedia, 13

Printed in the United States 6739

Table of Contents

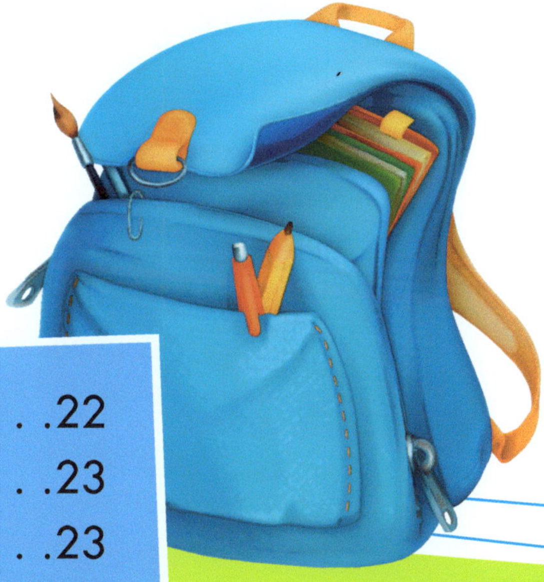

Time for School

A bell rings.

It's time for school!

Who helps kids at school?

SCHOOL BUS

Helpers at School

The principal runs the school.

She is in charge.

A teacher helps Ava learn.

Ava writes new words.

Liam tries to add numbers.

The teacher is busy.

A teacher's aide helps Liam.

Emma wants to read about cats. A librarian helps her find the right books.

B
H

Ouch!

Mason is hurt.

A nurse cares for him.

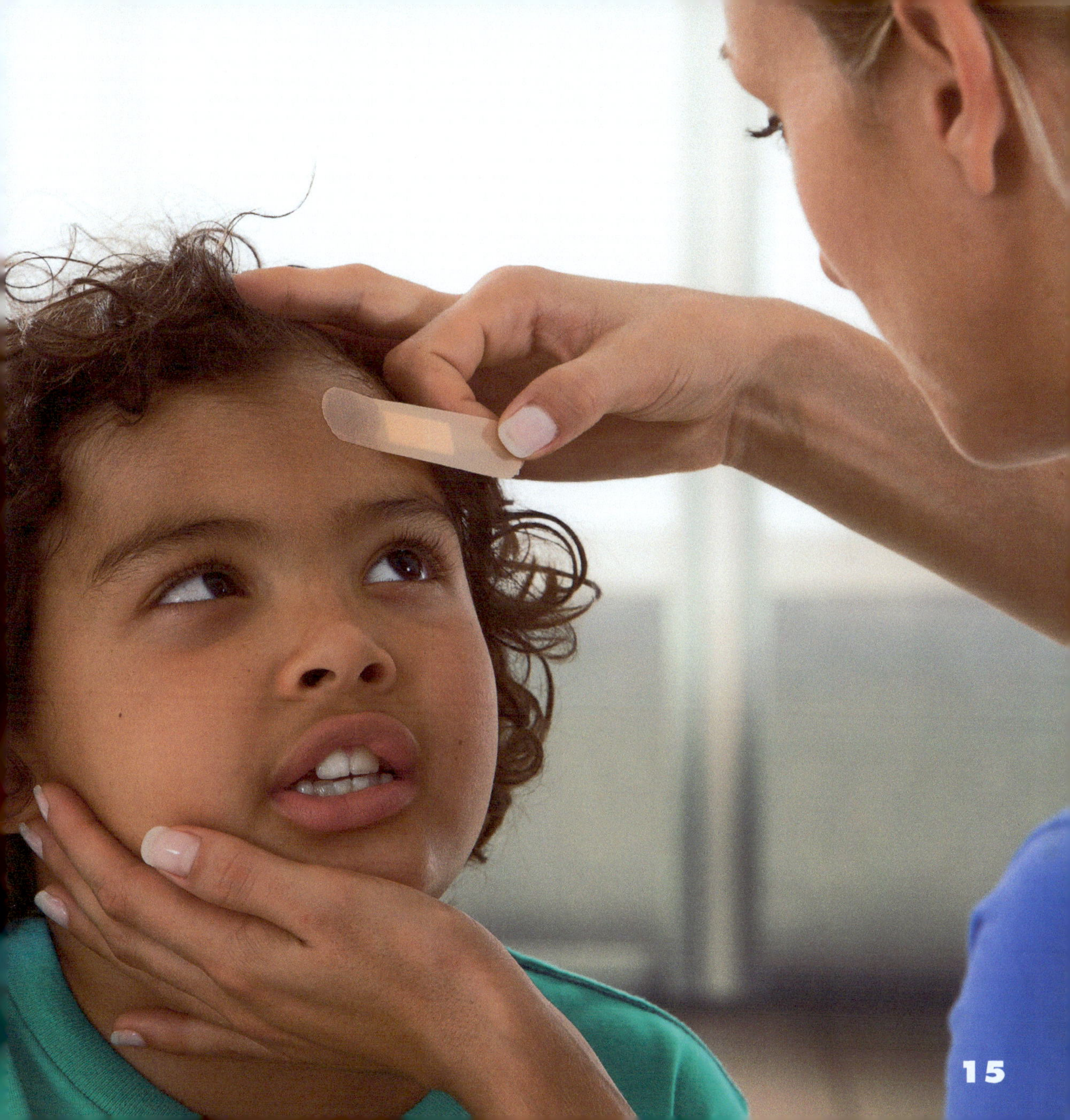

Noah is sad.

A counselor listens.

She helps him feel better.

What a mess!

A janitor cleans up.

CAUTION
ACHTUNG
ATTENTION
CUIDADO

Many helpers work at a school. They help kids learn and grow.

Glossary

counselor—a person who helps people during hard times

janitor—a person who cleans buildings and makes repairs

librarian—a person who helps people find books and information

nurse—a person who takes care of people who are sick or hurt

principal—the leader of a public school

teacher—a person who helps students learn

teacher's aide—a person who helps teachers and students

Read More

De Nijs, Erika. *A Teacher's Job.* Community Workers. New York: Cavendish Square Publishing, 2016.

Kidde, Rita. *What Does a Janitor Do?* Jobs in My School. New York: PowerKids Press, 2015.

Murray, Julie. *Principals.* Going to Work. Edina, Minn.: ABDO Publishing, 2011.

Internet Sites

FactHound offers a safe, fun way to find Internet sites related to this book. All of the sites on FactHound have been researched by our staff.

Here's all you do:
Visit *www.facthound.com*
Type in this code: 9781515724001

Index